D0864019

The Heights of Macchu Picchu

Alturas de Macchu Picchu

PABLO NERUDA

The Heights of Macchu Picchu

TRANSLATED BY TOMÁS Q. MORÍN

COPPER CANYON PRESS

PORT TOWNSEND, WASHINGTON

© Fundacion Pablo Neruda, 2015

Translation copyright 2015 by Tomás Q. Morín

All rights reserved.

Printed in the United States of America

Cover art: *Machu Picchu Houses,* ©Hanis/istockphoto.com

Copper Canyon Press is in residence at Fort Worden State
Park in Port Townsend, Washington, under the auspices of
Centrum. Centrum is a gathering place for artists and creative
thinkers from around the world, students of all ages and
backgrounds, and audiences seeking extraordinary cultural
enrichment.

LIBRARY OF CONGRESS CATALOGING-IN-PUBLICATION DATA

Neruda, Pablo, 1904–1973, author.
[Alturas de Macchu Picchu. English]
The Heights of Macchu Picchu / Pablo Neruda ;
translated by Tomás Q. Morín.
pages cm
ISBN 978-1-55659-444-1 (paperback)
I. Morín, Tomás Q., translator. II. Title.

PQ8097.N4A7513 2014
861'.62—dc23

2014027885
98765432 FIRST PRINTING

Copper Canyon Press
Post Office Box 271
Port Townsend, Washington 98368
www.coppercanyonpress.org

CONTENTS

ACKNOWLEDGMENTS

Many thanks to the editors who published selections of this
poem in their magazines:

The American Poetry Review: VI, VIII
Narrative: IV

TRANSLATOR'S ACKNOWLEDGMENTS

A thousand thanks to Eduardo González, Eva Teba Fernández, Luisa Muradyan, Dara Barnat, Traci Brimhall, and Antonio Ruiz-Camacho, all of whom helped me to test both my English and Spanish ears against their own. Without your help, I would no doubt feel less confident about the choices I made. Michael, Tonaya, George, Fred, Kelly, and interns far and wide: mil gracias. Your faith and perseverance brought this book to life. A hearty thank-you to D'Andra Luna for encouraging me to translate and for becoming friends with a certain Peruvian whose name I still can't remember. To Micah Ruelle, without whose fierce cheerleading this project would have taken longer to complete, thank you. Thank you, Melissa Stein, for your keen eye. My endless gratitude to Maggie Blake and Erin Evans for their unwavering support over the years. The two of you are constant lights in my life, guiding me ever forward. And to Philip Levine, your faith and encouragement continue to buoy me.

In preparing the notes, the National Geographic Society's website and the following books were indispensable: *Ancient Inca* by Alan L. Kolata, *The Incas: New Perspectives* by Gordon F. McEwan, *Memoirs* by Pablo Neruda, and *Machu Picchu: A Citadel of the Incas* by Hiram Bingham, a Western scholar who, in 1911, was led by a guide to the "lost city" the indigenous people always knew was there. Lastly, this translation would not exist without the tireless work of all the translators who have worked to bring Pablo Neruda into English and, in so doing, proved that the impossible challenge of making a poem live in two languages is a task worth doing. It's an honor to join the conversation begun by all of you who came before me.

for Jackie Eugene Powell
in memoriam

I'm an accidental translator. In spite of spending six years traveling a road I expected would end one day in my becoming a Spanish professor, I was never interested in translating. My thinking was that my research and teaching would involve books written in their original language, not English. When I left this path to devote myself to poetry, I didn't give translating much thought because I assumed it would take as much time and effort as writing my own poems (which turned out to be true).

I first read *The Heights of Macchu Picchu* as an undergraduate. In my memory, which is often unreliable, I see myself holding the Nathaniel Tarn translation with the marvelous Guy Fleming cover: a mountain silhouetted in aqua against a black background, a purple tree bursting in the foreground like fireworks. The poem was stunning. Within the twelve tidy and classical Roman numeral sections, Neruda's wild imagination leaped from one arresting image to another. I didn't know it at the time, but it would be fifteen years before I would return to the poem.

In the summer of 2012, my ex-wife, who was away in Baltimore attending graduate school, kept mentioning a new friend she had made whom was from Peru. Because I could never remember his name, I did what I usually do when new people come into my life whom I can't remember, I gave him a nickname: Macchu Picchu. After a couple of weeks I had said "Macchu Picchu" so often, I decided I should reread the poem. Out of curiosity, I went back and forth between the Spanish and the English and found that sometimes Neruda's ambiguities or his music hadn't been transferred over into English. Not wanting to cast a stone from a glass house, I decided to try my hand at the first stanza. That stanza led to the next and the next until, before I knew it, I was caught in the poem's whirlpool of associations. A couple of weeks later, the first draft was done.

My hope was to create a poem in English that would retain the power and majesty of the original. To this end, when I encountered all the obstacles translators wrestle with (music, syntax, tone, idiom), I tried to imagine what choices Neruda would have made had he been born in Topeka or Miami or any other U.S. city and thus been a native speaker of English. I let this Neruda guide me, especially when straying from the original was the only way to create a strong poem in English.

At the heart of the poem is the journey of a disillusioned man who struggles with feeling disconnected from people and nature. Lonely and lost in his own misery, he climbs up to the lost city of the Inca. Instead of finding comfort in that ancient citadel that has withstood the test of time, he finds reminders of pain and death. While the city's architecture stands as a testament to the genius of the Inca, its stones are a monument to the workers who built it. In the face of this great suffering, the poet finds the kinship he has been seeking. *The Heights of Macchu Picchu* is a chant for the broken and forgotten victims of American empires, whether they are English, Spanish, or Incan. Ultimately, the poem is not only an accounting of humankind's hunger for power and conquest but also a blueprint for empathy.

TOMÁS Q. MORÍN

The Heights of Macchu Picchu

Alturas de Macchu Picchu

I

Del aire al aire, como una red vacía,
iba yo entre las calles y la atmósfera, llegando y despidiendo,
en el advenimiento del otoño la moneda extendida
de las hojas, y entre la primavera y las espigas,
lo que el más grande amor, como dentro de un guante
que cae, nos entrega como una larga luna.

(Días de fulgor vivo en la intemperie
de los cuerpos: aceros convertidos
al silencio del ácido:
noches deshilachadas hasta la última harina:
estambres agredidos de la patria nupcial.)

Alguien que me esperó entre los violines
encontró un mundo como una torre enterrada
hundiendo su espiral más abajo de todas
las hojas de color de ronco azufre:
más abajo, en el oro de la geología,
como una espada envuelta en meteoros,
hundí la mano turbulenta y dulce
en lo más genital de lo terrestre.

Puse la frente entre las olas profundas,
descendí como gota entre la paz sulfúrica,
y, como un ciego, regresé al jazmín
de la gastada primavera humana.

I

Cast and cast, like an empty net through air,
I went through the streets and the atmosphere, arriving and departing,
the crowning of autumn brought the free coins
of its leaves, and between spring and its spears of wheat,
there waits, like a heavy moon inside a glove
that falls, what the greatest love grants us all.

(On radiant days, I live in the elements
of bodies: steel backbones are converted
to the silence of acid:
nights are ground down to their last grain:
unraveled threads of the nuptial land.)

Someone who waited for me among the violins
encountered a world like a buried tower
winding its spire even lower than all
the leaves the color of hoarse sulfur:
farther down, in the geologic womb,
like a sword wrapped in meteors,
I sank my muddy and gentle hand
into the precious treasure of the earth.

I dipped my forehead between the deep waves,
I ran like a single drop in peaceful sulfur,
and, like a blind man, returned to the jasmine
of our depleted human spring.

II

Si la flor a la flor entrega el alto germen
y la roca mantiene su flor diseminada
en su golpeado traje de diamante y arena,
el hombre arruga el pétalo de la luz que recoge
en los determinados manantiales marinos
y taladra el metal palpitante en sus manos.
Y pronto, entre la ropa y el humo, sobre la mesa hundida,
como una barajada cantidad, queda el alma:
cuarzo y desvelo, lágrimas en el océano
como estanques de frío: pero aún
mátala y agonízala con papel y con odio,
sumérgela en la alfombra cotidiana, desgárrala
entre las vestiduras hostiles del alambre.

No: por los corredores, aire, mar o caminos,
quién guarda sin puñal (como las encarnadas
amapolas) su sangre? La cólera ha extenuado
la triste mercancía del vendedor de seres,
y, mientras en la altura del ciruelo, el rocío
desde mil años deja su carta transparente
sobre la misma rama que lo espera, oh corazón, oh frente triturada
entre las cavidades del otoño.

Cuántas veces en las calles de invierno de una ciudad o en
un autobús o un barco en el crepúsculo, o en la soledad
más espesa, la de la noche de fiesta, bajo el sonido
de sombras y campanas, en la misma gruta del placer humano,

II

While a flower gives its seed to another flower
and the rock nourishes their offspring
on its battered suit of diamond and sand,
man crumples the petal of light he harvests
in the appointed wellsprings of the sea
and drills the trembling metal in his hands.
Before long, between clothes and smoke, on the sunken table
like a jumbled deck of cards, the soul:
quartz and insomnia, tears in the ocean
like cold puddles: go ahead and kill
the soul and torture it with paper and hate,
bury it under a cheap carpet, tear it
between the hostile clothes of wire.

No: on the byways of air, sea, or land,
who guards without a knife (like bloody
poppies) his life? Rage has depleted
the sad merchandise of the slave trader,
meanwhile atop the plum tree, the dew
a thousand years ago left its clear calling card
on the very branch waiting for it, O heart, O brow crushed
between the cavities of autumn.

How many times on a city's winter streets or on
a bus or a boat at twilight, or in the deepest
loneliness of a festive night, under the sound
of shadows and bells, in the very cave of human pleasure,

me quise detener a buscar la eterna veta insondable
que antes toqué en la piedra o en el relámpago que el beso desprendía.

(Lo que en el cereal como una historia amarilla
de pequeños pechos preñados va repitiendo un número
que sin cesar es ternura en las capas germinales,
y que, idéntica siempre, se desgrana en marfil
y lo que en el agua es patria transparente, campana
desde la nieve aislada hasta las olas sangrientas.)

No pude asir sino un racimo de rostros o de máscaras
precipitadas, como anillos de oro vacío,
como ropas dispersas hijas de un otoño rabioso
que hiciera temblar el miserable árbol de las razas asustadas.

No tuve sitio donde descansar la mano
y que, corriente como agua de manantial encadenado,
o firme como grumo de antracita, o cristal,
hubiera devuelto el calor o el frío de mi mano extendida.
Qué era el hombre? En qué parte de su conversación abierta
entre los almacenes y los silbidos, en cuál de sus movimientos metálicos
vivía lo indestructible, lo imperecedero, la vida?

did I almost stop and look for the endless eternal vein
I once felt in a stone or in the lightning of a kiss.

(What lives in wheat like a yellow history
of petite, pregnant breasts repeats an endless
formula tenderly in the germinal layer
that, always in the same way, drops its ivory grains,
and that which is a transparent country in water, clangs
from the lonely snow down to the bloody waves.)

I could not grasp anything but a cluster of faces
or slapdash masks, like rings of worthless gold,
like scattered clothes, the children of a furious autumn
that shook the poor tree of the frightened races.

There was no place for my hand to rest
that was as fluid as water from a harnessed spring,
or hard as a lump of coal or crystal,
that would have returned the warmth or cool of my open hand.
What was man? In which part of his debates
among his stores and whistles, in which of his robotic movements
lived the indestructible, the eternal, life?

III

El ser como el maíz se desgranaba en el inacabable
granero de los hechos perdidos, de los acontecimientos
miserables, del uno al siete, al ocho,
y no una muerte, sino muchas muertes llegaba a cada uno:
cada día una muerte pequeña, polvo, gusano, lámpara
que se apaga en el lodo del suburbio, una pequeña muerte de
     alas gruesas
entraba en cada hombre como una corta lanza
y era el hombre asediado del pan o del cuchillo,
el ganadero: el hijo de los puertos, o el capitán oscuro del arado,
o el roedor de las calles espesas:
todos desfallecieron esperando su muerte, su corta muerte diaria:
y su quebranto aciago de cada día era
como una copa negra que bebían temblando.

III

Men were threshed like maize in the bottomless
granary of deeds no one remembers, of moments
covering the full spectrum of misery, and beyond,
and not only one death, but many deaths came to each man:
each day a tiny death, dust, worm, a lamp
that flickers out in the mud of the suburbs, a tiny death on
  rough wings
pierced each man like a short lance
and thus was he menaced by the bread or the knife,
the cattle rancher: the child of seaports, or the dark captain of
  the plow,
or the rodent of the filthy streets:
they all despaired waiting for death, their short daily death:
and their grinding doom was each day
like a black cup from which they drank trembling.

IV

La poderosa muerte me invitó muchas veces:
era como la sal invisible en las olas,
y lo que su invisible sabor diseminaba
era como mitades de hundimientos y altura
o vastas construcciones de viento y ventisquero.

Yo al férreo filo vine, a la angostura
del aire, a la mortaja de agricultura y piedra,
al estelar vacío de los pasos finales
y a la vertiginosa carretera espiral:
pero, ancho mar, oh muerte!, de ola en ola no vienes,
sino como un galope de claridad nocturna
o como los totales números de la noche.

Nunca llegaste a hurgar en el bolsillo, no era
posible tu visita sin vestimenta roja:
sin auroral alfombra de cercado silencio:
sin altos y enterrados patrimonios de lágrimas.

No pude amar en cada ser un árbol
con su pequeño otoño a cuestas (la muerte de mil hojas),
todas las falsas muertes y las resurrecciones
sin tierra, sin abismo:
quise nadar en las más anchas vidas,
en las más sueltas desembocaduras,
y cuando poco a poco el hombre fue negándome
y fue cerrando paso y puerta para que no tocaran
mis manos manantiales su inexistencia herida,
entonces fui por calle y calle y río y río,
y ciudad y ciudad y cama y cama,
y atravesó el desierto mi máscara salobre,

IV

Almighty death invited me many times:
it was like the hidden salt in waves,
and its invisible flavors tasted
like collapsing shipwrecks and summits
or vast structures made by wind and snowdrifts.

I came to the iron edge, to the thinness
of air, to the shroud of farms and stones,
the starry void of the final steps
before the dizzying spiral road:
but wide sea, O death!, you don't come in waves
but rather like clear twilight galloping
or like the infinite host of the night.

You never came to dig in our pockets, your visit
was not possible without a red dress:
without a dawn-lit field ringed in silence:
without towering or buried monuments of tears.

I couldn't love the tree in every soul
shouldering its own tiny autumn (a thousand leaves dying),
all of these false deaths and resurrections
without graves, without oblivion:
I wanted to swim in the fullest lives,
in the widest estuaries,
and when little by little men renounced me
and closed their doors and paths so the fountains
of my hands wouldn't touch their wounded existence,
I then went street by street and river by river,
city by city and bed by bed,
my salty mask crossing the wilderness,

y en las últimas casas humilladas, sin lámpara, sin fuego,
sin pan, sin piedra, sin silencio, solo,
rodé muriendo de mi propia muerte.

and in the last humiliated houses, without light, fire,
bread, stone, or silence, alone,
I doubled over, dying of my own death.

V

No eras tú, muerte grave, ave de plumas férreas,
la que el pobre heredero de las habitaciones
llevaba entre alimentos apresurados, bajo la piel vacía:
era algo, un pobre pétalo de cuerda exterminada:
un átomo del pecho que no vino al combate
o el áspero rocío que no cayó en la frente.
Era lo que no pudo renacer, un pedazo
de la pequeña muerte sin paz ni territorio:
un hueso, una campana que morían en él.
Yo levanté las vendas del yodo, hundí las manos
en los pobres dolores que mataban la muerte,
y no encontré en la herida sino una racha fría
que entraba por los vagos intersticios del alma.

V

It was not you, solemn death, bird of iron feathers,
that the poor heir of these rooms
carried in his hurried meals, under his hollow skin:
it was something, the clipped life of a pitiful petal:
an atom from the heart that never came to battle
or the harsh dew that never knew a brow.
It was what he could not resurrect, a part
of that homeless, tiny death that knows no peace:
a bone, a bell, which were dying in him.
I lifted the iodine bandages, plunged my hands
in the wretched sorrows that were killing death,
and found nothing in the wound but a cold wind
that slipped through the useless cracks in the soul.

VI

Entonces en la escala de la tierra he subido
entre la atroz maraña de las selvas perdidas
hasta ti, Macchu Picchu.
Alta ciudad de piedras escalares,
por fin morada del que lo terrestre
no escondió en las dormidas vestiduras.
En ti, como dos líneas paralelas,
la cuna del relámpago y del hombre
se mecían en un viento de espinas.

Madre de piedra, espuma de los cóndores.

Alto arrecife de la aurora humana.

Pala perdida en la primera arena.

Ésta fue la morada, éste es el sitio:
aquí los anchos granos del maíz ascendieron
y bajaron de nuevo como granizo rojo.

Aquí la hebra dorada salió de la vicuña
a vestir los amores, los túmulos, las madres,
el rey, las oraciones, los guerreros.

Aquí los pies del hombre descansaron de noche
junto a los pies del águila, en las altas guaridas
carniceras, y en la aurora
pisaron con los pies del trueno la niebla enrarecida,

VI

And then on the stairs of the earth I ascended
through the savage tangle of the lost jungles
to you, Macchu Picchu.
High city of stepped stones,
sanctuary at long last of what the earth
never hid away in its nightclothes.
In you, like two parallel lines,
the cradle of lightning and the cradle of man
were rocked by a wind of thorns.

Mother of stone, sperm of condors.

High stone road of the human dawn.

Lost shovel in the primordial sand.

This was the home, this was the place:
here the plump grains of maize climbed
and like red hail came back down again.

Here the vicuña gave the gold thread
to clothe love, tombs, mothers,
the king, prayers, warriors.

Here the feet of men rested at night
next to the feet of the eagle, in the high bloody
lairs, and at first light
they stepped with thunderous feet on the tense mist,

y tocaron las tierras y las piedras
hasta reconocerlas en la noche o la muerte.

Miro las vestiduras y las manos,
el vestigio del agua en la oquedad sonora,
la pared suavizada por el tacto de un rostro
que miró con mis ojos las lámparas terrestres,
que aceitó con mis manos las desaparecidas
maderas: porque todo, ropaje, piel, vasijas,
palabras, vino, panes,
se fue, cayó a la tierra.

Y el aire entró con dedos
de azahar sobre todos los dormidos:
mil años de aire, meses, semanas de aire,
de viento azul, de cordillera férrea,
que fueron como suaves huracanes de pasos
lustrando el solitario recinto de la piedra.

and then touched the earth and the stones
until they would have known them even at night or in
     death.

I stare at the clothes and hands,
the carvings of water in a sonorous hollow,
the wall rubbed smooth by the touch of a face
that with my eyes gazed at the earthly lights,
that with my hands oiled the vanished
planks: because everything, clothes, skin, dishes,
words, wine, breads,
went away, fell to the earth.

And the air came with its fingers
of orange blossom over all of the sleepers:
a thousand years of air, months, weeks of air,
of a blue wind, of an iron mountain ridge,
that was like a soft hurricane of footfalls
polishing the solitary site of stone.

VII

Muertos de un solo abismo, sombras de una hondonada,
la profunda, es así como al tamaño
de vuestra magnitud
vino la verdadera, la más abrasadora
muerte y desde las rocas taladradas,
desde los capiteles escarlata,
desde los acueductos escalares
os desplomasteis como en un otoño
en una sola muerte.
Hoy el aire vacío ya no llora,
ya no conoce vuestros pies de arcilla,
ya olvidó vuestros cántaros que filtraban el cielo
cuando lo derramaban los cuchillos del rayo,
y el árbol poderoso fue comido
por la niebla, y cortado por la racha.

Él sostuvo una mano que cayó de repente
desde la altura hasta el final del tiempo.
Ya no sois, manos de araña, débiles
hebras, tela enmarañada:
cuanto fuisteis cayó: costumbres, sílabas
raídas, máscaras de luz deslumbradora.

Pero una permanencia de piedra y de palabra:
la ciudad como un vaso se levantó en las manos
de todos, vivos, muertos, callados, sostenidos
de tanta muerte, un muro, de tanta vida un golpe

VII

Victims of a lonely abyss, shadows of a valley,
the deepest one, matching perfectly the size
of your magnitude,
the destroyer came, the most white-hot
death and from the carved rocks,
from the scarlet tops of columns,
from the stepped aqueducts
like a single death
in autumn you collapsed.
Today the empty air no longer mourns,
no longer recognizes your clay feet,
has forgotten your jugs that filtered the sky
when it was slit open by the knives of lightning,
and the mighty tree was devoured
by the fog and cut by the wind.

It held up against a hand that fell suddenly
from the heights to the end of time.
You are no more, hands of the spider, weak
threads, entangled web:
what you were fell away: customs, frayed
syllables, masks of dizzying light.

But stone and language are permanent:
like a cup the city was raised in the hands
of everyone, the living, the dead, the silent, built
upon so much death, a wall, out of so much life a smack

de pétalos de piedra: la rosa permanente, la morada:
este arrecife andino de colonias glaciales.

Cuando la mano de color de arcilla
se convirtió en arcilla, y cuando los pequeños párpados se cerraron
llenos de ásperos muros, poblados de castillos,
y cuando todo el hombre se enredó en su agujero,
quedó la exactitud enarbolada:
el alto sitio de la aurora humana:
la más alta vasija que contuvo el silencio:
una vida de piedra después de tantas vidas.

of stone petals: the eternal rose, our home:
this Andean road of glacial colonies.

When a hand the color of clay
became clay, and when tiny eyelids carrying rugged
walls and castle dwellers closed,
and when man was ensnared in his burrow,
only elevated exactitude was left:
this high place of our human dawn:
the highest vessel to contain our silence:
a life of stone after so many lives.

VIII

Sube conmigo, amor americano.

Besa conmigo las piedras secretas.
La plata torrencial del Urubamba
hace volar el polen a su copa amarilla.

Vuela el vacío de la enredadera,
la planta pétrea, la guirnalda dura
sobre el silencio del cajón serrano.
Ven, minúscula vida, entre las alas
de la tierra, mientras—cristal y frío, aire golpeado—
apartando esmeraldas combatidas,
oh agua salvaje, bajas de la nieve.

Amor, amor, hasta la noche abrupta,
desde el sonoro pedernal andino,
hacia la aurora de rodillas rojas,
contempla el hijo ciego de la nieve.

Oh, Wilkamayu de sonoros hilos,
cuando rompes tus truenos lineales
en blanca espuma, como herida nieve,
cuando tu vendaval acantilado
canta y castiga despertando al cielo,
qué idioma traes a la oreja apenas
desarraigada de tu espuma andina?

Quién apresó el relámpago del frío
y lo dejó en la altura encadenado,
repartido en sus lágrimas glaciales,
sacudido en sus rápidas espadas,

VIII

Rise with me, American love.

Kiss the secret stones with me.
The silver torrent of the Urubamba
flies the pollen to its golden cup.

It blows away the emptiness of the bindweed,
the stony plant, the stiff wreath
laid on the silence of the mountain coffin.
Come, minuscule life, upon the wings
of the earth, while—glassy and cold, pummeled air—
you move aside stubborn emeralds,
O savage water, you descend from the snow.

Love, love, even the short night
from the raucous Andean flint
to the red-kneed dawn
contemplates the blind son of the snow.

O Wilkamayu of loud streams,
when you crack your steady thunder
into a white foam, like wounded snow,
when your mountainous wind
sings and pounds the sky awake,
what language do you speak to the ear
just now freed from your Andean spume?

Who captured the cold's lightning bolt
and left it chained on the peaks,
broken down into its glacial tears,
frisked of its swift swords,

---

golpeando sus estambres aguerridos,
conducido en su cama de guerrero,
sobresaltado en su final de roca?

Qué dicen tus destellos acosados?
Tu secreto relámpago rebelde
antes viajó poblado de palabras?
Quién va rompiendo sílabas heladas,
idiomas negros, estandartes de oro,
bocas profundas, gritos sometidos,
en tus delgadas aguas arteriales?

Quién va cortando párpados florales
que vienen a mirar desde la tierra?
Quién precipita los racimos muertos
que bajan en tus manos de cascada
a desgranar su noche desgranada
en el carbón de la geología?

Quién despeña la rama de los vínculos?
Quién otra vez sepulta los adioses?

Amor, amor, no toques la frontera,
ni adores la cabeza sumergida:
deja que el tiempo cumpla su estatura
en su salón de manantiales rotos,
y, entre el agua veloz y las murallas,
recoge el aire del desfiladero,
las paralelas láminas del viento,
el canal ciego de las cordilleras,
el áspero saludo del rocío,

striking its battle-tested stamens,
laid in its warrior's bed,
startled by this rocky end?

What do your tortured sparks say?
Did your hidden, rebel lightning bolt
ever carry words on its journeys?
Who is putting an end to frozen syllables,
dark languages, golden banners,
bottomless mouths, muffled cries,
in your narrow arterial waters?

Who is cutting the eyelids of flowers
that have come to watch you from the earth?
Who will scatter the dead bouquets,
shedding their night that was shucked
in the carbon of geology
as they fall from your cascading hands?

Who flings the branch over a cliff, away from its bonds?
Who is entombing our farewells yet again?

Love, love, do not touch the border
or adore the buried head:
let time run its course
in its hall of shattered wellsprings,
and, between the swift water and the walls,
the head will gather its air from the canyon,
the parallel capes of the wind,
the blind canal of the mountain ridge,
the grumpy greeting of the dew,

y sube, flor a flor, por la espesura,
pisando la serpiente despeñada.

En la escarpada zona, piedra y bosque,
polvo de estrellas verdes, selva clara,
Mantur estalla como un lago vivo
o como un nuevo piso del silencio.

Ven a mi propio ser, al alba mía,
hasta las soledades coronadas.
El reino muerto vive todavía.

Y en el Reloj la sombra sanguinaria
del cóndor cruza como una nave negra.

---

and climb, flower by flower, through the thicket,
trampling the castaway serpent.

In the sloped zone of rock and forest,
the dust of green stars, clear jungle,
the Mantur valley explodes like a living lake
or like a new footstep from silence.

Come to me my proper self, to my dawn,
even unto my crowned solitudes.
The kingdom of death still lives.

And over the Sundial the cruel shadow
of the condor crosses like a black ship.

Águila sideral, viña de bruma.
Bastión perdido, cimitarra ciega.
Cinturón estrellado, pan solemne.
Escala torrencial, párpado inmenso.
Túnica triangular, polen de piedra.
Lámpara de granito, pan de piedra.
Serpiente mineral, rosa de piedra.
Nave enterrada, manantial de piedra.
Caballo de la luna, luz de piedra.
Escuadra equinoccial, vapor de piedra.
Geometría final, libro de piedra.
Témpano entre las ráfagas labrado.
Madrépora del tiempo sumergido.
Muralla por los dedos suavizada.
Techumbre por las plumas combatida.
Ramos de espejo, bases de tormenta.
Tronos volcados por la enredadera.
Régimen de la garra encarnizada.
Vendaval sostenido en la vertiente.
Inmóvil catarata de turquesa.
Campana patriarcal de los dormidos.
Argolla de las nieves dominadas.
Hierro acostado sobre sus estatuas.
Inaccesible temporal cerrado.
Manos de puma, roca sanguinaria.
Torre sombrera, discusión de nieve.
Noche elevada en dedos y raíces.
Ventana de las nieblas, paloma endurecida.
Planta nocturna, estatua de los truenos.
Cordillera esencial, techo marino.
Arquitecto de águilas perdidas.

Astral eagle, vine of sea mist.
Lost bastion, blind scimitar.
Cosmic belt, solemn bread.
Torrential ladder, immense eyelid.
Triangular tunic, pollen of stone.
Granite lamp, bread of stone.
Mineral serpent, rose of stone.
Buried ship, wellspring of stone.
Horse of the moon, light of stone.
Equinoctial square, breath of stone.
Ultimate geometry, book of stone.
Ice floe between the carved storms.
White reef of submerged time.
Rampart worn smooth between fingers.
Vaulted roof assaulted by feathers.
Shards of a mirror, root of tempests.
Thrones knocked over by the vine.
Law of the bloody claw.
Storm stalled on the slope.
Immovable waterfall of turquoise.
Patriarchal bell of the sleepers.
Collar of the submissive snows.
Iron reclining on its statues.
Dark distant storm.
Paws of the puma, bloody rock.
Shadow tower, argument of snow.
Night elevated on fingers and roots.
Window of the mists, callous dove.
Nocturnal plant, statue of thunder.
Vital ridge, sea roof.
Architect of lost eagles.

Cuerda del cielo, abeja de la altura.
Nivel sangriento, estrella construida.
Burbuja mineral, luna de cuarzo.
Serpiente andina, frente de amaranto.
Cúpula del silencio, patria pura.
Novia del mar, árbol de catedrales.
Ramo de sal, cerezo de alas negras.
Dentadura nevada, trueno frío.
Luna arañada, piedra amenazante.
Cabellera del frío, acción del aire.
Volcán de manos, catarata oscura.
Ola de plata, dirección del tiempo.

Rope of the sky, bee of the peaks.
Bloody spirit level, engineered star.
Mineral bubble, moon of quartz.
Andean serpent, brow of amaranth.
Dome of silence, uncorrupt country.
Bride of the sea, tree of cathedrals.
Cluster of salt, black-winged cherry tree.
Snowy teeth, cold thunder.
Scratched moon, menacing stone.
Tresses of the cold, pose of the air.
Volcano of hands, dark waterfall.
Wave of silver, time's compass.

X

Piedra en la piedra, el hombre, dónde estuvo?
Aire en el aire, el hombre, dónde estuvo?
Tiempo en el tiempo, el hombre, dónde estuvo?
Fuiste también el pedacito roto
de hombre inconcluso, de águila vacía
que por las calles de hoy, que por las huellas,
que por las hojas del otoño muerto
va machacando el alma hasta la tumba?
La pobre mano, el pie, la pobre vida...
Los días de la luz deshilachada
en ti, como la lluvia
sobre las banderillas de la fiesta,
dieron pétalo a pétalo de su alimento oscuro
en la boca vacía?

        Hambre, coral del hombre,
hambre, planta secreta, raíz de los leñadores,
hambre, subió tu raya de arrecife
hasta estas altas torres desprendidas?

Yo te interrogo, sal de los caminos,
muéstrame la cuchara, déjame, arquitectura,
roer con un palito los estambres de piedra,
subir todos los escalones del aire hasta el vacío,
rascar la entraña hasta tocar el hombre.

Macchu Picchu, pusiste
piedra en la piedra, y en la base, harapo?
Carbón sobre carbón, y en el fondo la lágrima?
Fuego en el oro, y en él, temblando el rojo

X

Stone upon stone, but man, where was he?
Air upon air, but man, where was he?
Time upon time, but man, where was he?
Were you also the shattered piece
of the incomplete man, of the unfinished eagle,
who through your streets today, over your trails,
above the leaves from your dead autumn,
keeps crushing the soul all the way to its tomb?
The poor hand, the foot, the pitiful life...
Did the days of frayed light
in you, like the rain
on the decorated darts of a bullfight,
feed their dark food, petal by petal,
into the empty mouth?
                              Hunger, man's coral reef,
hunger, hidden plant, root of the lumberjacks,
hunger, did your rough road climb
even to these high secluded towers?

I question you, salt of the roads,
show me the spoon, allow me, architecture,
to poke with a stick the petrified stamens,
to climb every step of air up to the emptiness,
to scrape your heart until I touch a man.

Macchu Picchu, did you place
stone upon stone, and at the base, tattered clothes?
Coal upon coal, and at the bottom, tears?
Fire to gold, and within it, trembling, the red

goterón de la sangre?
Devuélveme el esclavo que enterraste!
Sacude de las tierras el pan duro
del miserable, muéstrame los vestidos
del siervo y su ventana.
Dime cómo durmió cuando vivía.
Dime si fue su sueño
ronco, entreabierto, como un hoyo negro
hecho por la fatiga sobre el muro.
El muro, el muro! Si sobre su sueño
gravitó cada piso de piedra, y si cayó bajo ella
como bajo una luna, con el sueño!
Antigua América, novia sumergida,
también tus dedos,
al salir de la selva hacia el alto vacío de los dioses,
bajo los estandartes nupciales de la luz y el decoro,
mezclándose al trueno de los tambores y de las lanzas,
también, también tus dedos,
los que la rosa abstracta y la línea del frío, los
que el pecho sangriento del nuevo cereal trasladaron
hasta la tela de materia radiante, hasta las duras cavidades,
también, también, América enterrada, guardaste en lo más bajo
en el armago intestino, como un águila, el hambre?

large drop of blood?
Give me back the slave you buried!
Release from the ground the stale bread
of the beggar, show me the clothes
for the servant and his window.
Tell me how he slept when he was alive.
Tell me whether his sleep was
raucous, agape, like a black hole
made by fatigue on the wall.
The wall, the wall! Whether over his sleep
loomed every stone layer, and whether he fell under it
as if beneath a moon, due to his sleepiness!
Ancient America, buried bride,
your fingers also,
upon leaving the jungle for the empty height of the gods,
under the nuptial banners of light and decorum,
blending with the thunder of drums and spears,
likewise, your fingers also,
the ones that the abstract rose and the edge of cold, those
that the bloodstained slope of the new crop transferred
to the radiant cloth, to the hardened cavities,
likewise, also, buried America, did you stow hunger
in the deepest place, in your bitter gut, like an eagle?

XI

A través del confuso esplendor,
a través de la noche de piedra, déjame hundir la mano
y deja que en mí palpite, como un ave mil años prisionera,
el viejo corazón del olvidado!
Déjame olvidar hoy esta dicha, que es más ancha que el mar,
porque el hombre es más ancho que el mar y que sus islas,
y hay que caer en él como en un pozo para salir del fondo
con un ramo de agua secreta y de verdades sumergidas.
Déjame olvidar, ancha piedra, la proporción poderosa,
la trascendente medida, las piedras del panal,
y de la escuadra déjame hoy resbalar
la mano sobre la hipotenusa de áspera sangre y cilicio.
Cuando, como una herradura de élitros rojos, el cóndor furibundo
me golpea las sienes en el orden del vuelo
y el huracán de plumas carniceras barre el polvo sombrío
de las escalinatas diagonales, no veo a la bestia veloz,
no veo el ciego ciclo de sus garras,
veo el antiguo ser, servidor, el dormido
en los campos, veo un cuerpo, mil cuerpos, un hombre, mil mujeres,
bajo la racha negra, negros de lluvia y noche,
con la piedra pesada de la estatua:
Juan Cortapiedras, hijo de Wiracocha,
Juan Comefrío, hijo de estrella verde,
Juan Piesdescalzos, nieto de la turquesa,
sube a nacer conmigo, hermano.

XI

Through the confusing splendor,
through the night of stone, let me plunge my hand
and let throb inside me, like a bird imprisoned a thousand years,
the old heart of the forsaken!
Let me forget today this joy, which is wider than the sea,
because man is greater than the sea and all its islands,
and we must fall into him as into a well, to emerge from the bottom
with a bouquet of secret water and sunken truths.
Let me forget, colossal rock, the titanic scale,
the transcendent breadth, the stones of the honeycomb,
and from the plaza let me today slide
my hand over the hair shirt and bloodstained hypotenuse.
When, like a horseshoe of red-beetle wings, the furious condor
pummels my head as it takes flight
and a hurricane of hungry feathers sweeps the somber dust
from the diagonal stairs, I do not see the swift beast,
I do not see the blind cycle of its talons,
I see the ancient man, a servant, the one sleeping
in the fields, I see a body, a thousand bodies, a man, a thousand
        women,
under an ill wind, darkened by rain and night,
with the heavy stone of a statue:
Juan Stonecutter, son of Wiracocha,
Juan Coldeater, son of a green star,
Juan Barefeet, grandson of turquoise,
rise to be born with me, brother.

Sube a nacer conmigo, hermano.

Dame la mano desde la profunda
zona de tu dolor diseminado.
No volverás del fondo de las rocas.
No volverás del tiempo subterráneo.
No volverá tu voz endurecida.
No volverán tus ojos taladrados.
Mírame desde el fondo de la tierra,
labrador, tejedor, pastor callado:
domador de guanacos tutelares:
albañil del andamio desafiado:
aguador de las lágrimas andinas:
joyero de los dedos machacados:
agricultor temblando en la semilla:
alfarero en tu greda derramado:
traed a la copa de esta nueva vida
vuestros viejos dolores enterrados.
Mostradme vuestra sangre y vuestro surco,
decidme: aquí fui castigado,
porque la joya no brilló o la tierra
no entregó a tiempo la piedra o el grano:
señaladme la piedra en que caísteis
y la madera en que os crucificaron,
encendedme los viejos pedernales,
las viejas lámparas, los látigos pegados
a través de los siglos en las llagas
y las hachas de brillo ensangrentado.
Yo vengo a hablar por vuestra boca muerta.
A través de la tierra juntad todos
los silenciosos labios derramados

XII

Rise to be born with me, brother.

Give me your hand out of the deepest
field your sorrows have sown.
You will not return from under the rocks.
You will not return from subterranean time.
You will not regain your hardened voice.
You will not recover your drilled eyes.
Watch me from the depths of the earth,
laborer, weaver, shy shepherd:
trainer of guardian guanacos:
mason of the dangerous scaffold:
water carrier of Andean tears:
jeweler of crushed fingers:
farmer trembling in the seed:
potter in your poured clay:
bring to the cup of this new life
all of your old buried pains.
Show me your blood and your furrow,
tell me: here I was punished,
because a jewel did not sparkle or the earth
did not submit on time its gem or grain:
point out the stone on which you fell
and the wood upon which you were crucified,
illuminate for me the old flints,
the old lamps, the lashes stuck
to your wounds throughout the centuries
and the axes shiny with your blood.
I come to speak through your dead mouth.
Throughout the earth gather all
the scattered, quiet lips

y desde el fondo habladme toda esta larga noche
como si yo estuviera con vosotros anclado,
contadme todo, cadena a cadena,
eslabón a eslabón, y paso a paso,
afilad los cuchillos que guardasteis,
ponedlos en mi pecho y en mi mano,
como un río de rayos amarillos,
como un río de tigres enterrados,
y dejadme llorar, horas, días, años,
edades ciegas, siglos estelares.

Dadme el silencio, el agua, la esperanza.

Dadme la lucha, el hierro, los volcanes.

Apegadme los cuerpos como imanes.

Acudid a mis venas y a mi boca.

Hablad por mis palabras y mi sangre.

and from the deep talk with me all this long night
as if I were bound with you.
Tell me everything, chain by chain,
link by link, and step by step,
sharpen the knives you saved,
place them in my chest and in my hand,
like a river of yellow thunderbolts,
like a river of buried jaguars,
and let me cry, hours, days, years,
blind ages, cosmic centuries.

Hand me silence, water, hope.

Hand me the struggle, the iron, the volcanoes.

Stick the bodies to me like magnets.

Hurry to my veins and my mouth.

Speak through my words and my blood.

Notes

Since 1950 "The Heights of Macchu Picchu" has been the second section of Neruda's epic *Canto general*, a book twelve years in the making, in which he chronicles the past, present, and future of the Americas. It is historical and mythological, lyrical and narrative, and furthers the journey of the pilgrim we meet in "The Heights of Macchu Picchu."

Most everyone spells Macchu with one *c*, while Neruda uses two. Enrico Mario Santí, in the introduction to his edition of Neruda's *Canto general* (general song), writes that the extra *c* gave the name Macchu Picchu twelve letters, and thus created symmetry with the twelve cantos of the poem. The truth is we don't know why he chose this spelling. Neruda uses a double *c* when he refers to the ruins in his memoir, *Confieso que he vivido* (I confess that I have lived). What is clear is he was consistent in his spelling, whether he was writing about the ruins or his poem. While "Machu Picchu" is the standard spelling, "Macchu Picchu" is by no means wrong. As Santí reminds us, Quechua was not a written language, thus there is no one correct way to spell the name of the ruins.

The fourth edition of *Obras completas* (Collected works), published in Buenos Aires by Losada in 1973, contains Neruda's last corrections to his work. This translation is based on that text.

VI

Macchu Picchu: At an elevation of almost 8,000 feet above sea level, the Incan ruins are located between two mountains in the Andes. Many archaeologists believe the site was not a city, but rather one of the country estates built by Emperor Pachacuti in the fifteenth century.

condor: Sacred to the Inca and believed to travel between the earth and the world of the gods. The Temple of the Condor and the shape of a flying condor the ruins make when seen from above attest to the bird's importance to the Inca.

vicuña: A smaller, undomesticated relative of the llama, prized for its extremely fine wool.

VII

victims: The Inca did not have a system of slavery. Instead, they used a work/tax system known as *mit'a,* which required citizens to answer drafts for military service, and for labor in the form of farming, mining, and construction.

aqueducts: The Inca employed a sophisticated system of canals, aqueducts, and basins to carry water from high elevations to irrigate fields and to use in homes.

VIII

American: In his memoirs, Neruda recounts how his understanding of who and what he was expanded while visiting the ruins of Macchu Picchu: "I felt Chilean, Peruvian, American." It is important to note, when Neruda says American, he does not mean "of the United States." Rather, he refers to a New World identity that is not European, and that stretches across both North and South America.

Urubamba: A dangerous tributary of the Amazon River, snaking some 4,000 feet below Macchu Picchu. According to some experts, the Inca believed the Urubamba was a manifestation of the Milky Way, the great river of stars they followed in the sky.

Wilkamayu: The Incan name for the Urubamba. The name also means "sacred river."

Sundial: The Intihuatana ("Hitching Post of the Sun") stone was used as an altar, as well as to mark the winter solstice with its shadow.

XI

plaza: The ruins of Macchu Picchu contain two plazas: the Central Plaza and the Sacred Plaza; the latter was a site for religious rituals and ceremonies.

hair shirt: Also known as a cilice, it is a rough undergarment made from cloth or animal skin, meant to irritate the skin with the purpose of demonstrating religious conviction.

hypotenuse: May be a reference to the Intihuatana stone (see section VIII) located in the Sacred Plaza.

Wiracocha (usually spelled "Viracocha"): A pre-Incan deity the Inca adopted, he was the supreme creator of the sun, moon, stars, and all of nature—including humans, whom he made spring to life from the stones of the earth.

XII

guanaco: Another small, undomesticated relative of the llama.

About the Author

Pablo Neruda (1904–1973) was born Neftalí Ricardo Reyes Basoalto in Parral, Chile. As a young man he served for well over a decade as consul in Europe and East Asia. He lived in hiding and exile from 1947 to 1952 due to his support of workers protesting government mistreatment. He made a home in Isla Negra upon his return to Chile. His output was immense, and his collected works number well over 3,000 pages. In awarding Pablo Neruda the Nobel Prize in Literature for 1971, the Nobel Committee extolled his "poetry that with the action of an elemental force brings alive a continent's destiny and dreams."

About the Translator

Tomás Q. Morín is the author of *A Larger Country*, winner of the APR/ Honickman First Book Prize, and is co-editor with Mari L'Esperance of *Coming Close: Forty Essays on Philip Levine*. His poems have appeared in *Poetry*, *New England Review*, *Slate*, *The Threepenny Review*, *Boulevard*, and *Narrative*.

Poetry is vital to language and living. Since 1972, Copper Canyon Press has published extraordinary poetry from around the world to engage the imaginations and intellects of readers, writers, booksellers, librarians, teachers, students, and donors.

WE ARE GRATEFUL FOR THE MAJOR SUPPORT PROVIDED BY:

THE PAUL G. ALLEN
FAMILY FOUNDATION

Lannan

THE MAURER FAMILY
FOUNDATION

A&

OFFICE OF ARTS & CULTURE
SEATTLE

WASHINGTON STATE
ARTS COMMISSION

Anonymous

John Branch

Diana Broze

Beroz Ferrell & The Point, LLC

Janet and Les Cox

Mimi Gardner Gates

Gull Industries, Inc.
on behalf of William and Ruth True

Linda Gerrard and Walter Parsons

Mark Hamilton and Suzie Rapp

Carolyn and Robert Hedin

Steven Myron Holl

Lakeside Industries, Inc.
on behalf of Jeanne Marie Lee

Maureen Lee and Mark Busto

Brice Marden

Ellie Mathews and Carl Youngmann as
The North Press

H. Stewart Parker

Penny and Jerry Peabody

John Phillips and Anne O'Donnell

Joseph C. Roberts

Cynthia Lovelace Sears and Frank Buxton

The Seattle Foundation

Dan Waggoner

Charles and Barbara Wright

The dedicated interns and faithful volunteers of Copper Canyon Press

TO LEARN MORE ABOUT UNDERWRITING COPPER CANYON PRESS TITLES,
PLEASE CALL 360-385-4925 EXT. 103

OTHER BOOKS BY PABLO NERUDA
FROM COPPER CANYON PRESS

World's End
The Hands of Day
Still Another Day
The Separate Rose
Winter Garden
Stones of the Sky
The Sea and the Bells
The Yellow Heart
The Book of Questions

The Chinese character for poetry is made up of two parts:
"word" and "temple." It also serves as pressmark for
Copper Canyon Press.

The poem is set in Sabon.
Book design and composition by Phil Kovacevich.

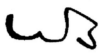

Copper Canyon Press wishes to thank the
Witter Bynner Foundation for Poetry for their generous support
of the publication of *The Heights of Macchu Picchu*.